a gift for:

from:

Easter A to Z: Fun Facts for Kids!

Text © 2006 by Snapdragon Editorial Group
Manuscript written and prepared by SnapdragonGroup℠ Editorial Services

Design © 2006 by Karen Phillips [mtudesign.net]

ISBN: 1-59530-107-0

Published by Hallmark Books, a division of Hallmark Cards, Inc.,
Kansas City, MO 64141

Visit us on the Web at www.Hallmark.com.

Printed and bound in China

BOK6055

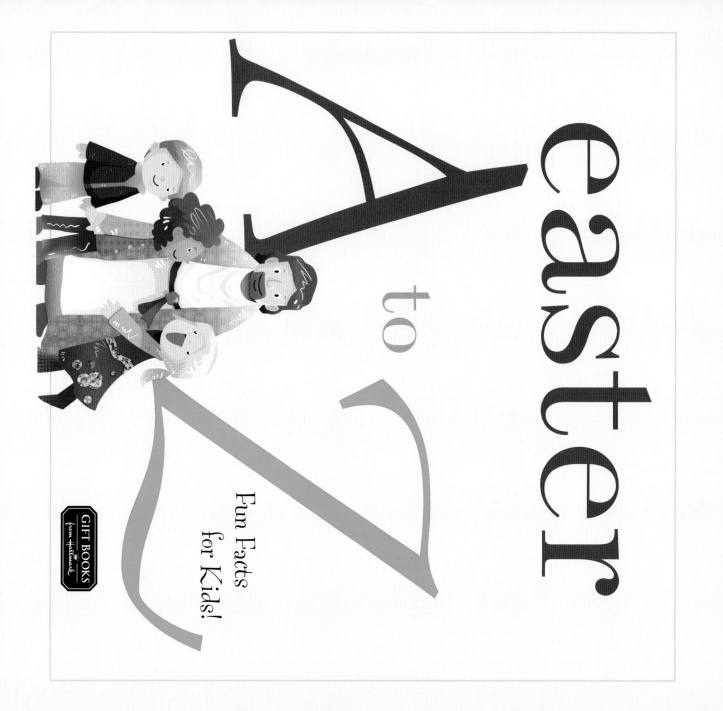

easter

A to Z

Fun Facts for Kids!

GIFT BOOKS from Hallmark

Introduction

If you're reading this book, chances are that Easter is coming soon! During the Easter season, people around the world remember how **Jesus** was crucified, but then miraculously came to life more than **2,000** years ago. They think about what **Jesus'** resurrection meant to those who lived in Jesus' time—and what it means to us today.

After you finish this book, you will understand some of the mysteries and unusual customs surrounding Easter. And we hope you'll love and respect **Jesus** more than ever, too! So let's learn about this important holiday—it's fun, and it's as easy as A, B, C . . .

is for Angels

Angels have played a key role in many important Bible events, and Easter is no exception. For example, angels greeted some people who came to Jesus' tomb after He was crucified—people who wanted to pay their respects to Jesus.

But instead of finding Him lying dead in a grave, these people saw angels — angels who greeted them with the happy news that Jesus had risen from the dead, showing the world that He has power even over death! And the power to forgive people for everything they have done wrong.

By the way, according to legend, angels were so happy that Jesus rose from the dead that they played catch with the huge stone that sealed His tomb. That stone weighed about 2,000 pounds, about as much as your family car! Did you know angels were so strong?

B is for Basket

Ever wonder why Easter baskets are part of Easter celebrations? Many people believe that this tradition sprung from the days when people from some churches put their Easter dinners in a basket, then carried them to church so that the leader of the church could bless the food before it was eaten. (It gives new meaning to the term "take-out food," doesn't it?)

Others think the concept of the Easter basket was inspired by the Old Testament custom of farmers bringing their first crops to the temple as an offering to God. So this year, when you pick through that funky fake grass, looking for your favorite flavor jelly-beans, remember that the Easter basket has meaning beyond being a candy holder.

is for Candle

You probably see lots of candles during the Christmas season, but look around during Easter, and you'll probably see candles burning then too.

For example, on Holy Saturday (the day before Easter Sunday), some churches hold an evening service and turn out all the lights, plunging everyone into darkness.

Then a priest or pastor lights one tall candle, representing the risen Christ. This candle is used to light other candles, held by worshippers. This act symbolizes the spreading of Jesus' light throughout the world.

This Easter season, when you see a candle glowing, remember how Jesus is your light. His love gives you comfort, and His words and actions teach you how to live a good, happy life.

D is for Donkey

Before the painful time leading up to His death, Jesus rode into Jerusalem on a young donkey, sometimes called a colt or a foal. (You can learn more about this ride when you get to letters "T" and "Z." Why would Jesus, who was God's son and a king to many people, ride a lowly donkey, rather than a majestic war horse, the ride of choice for other leaders of Jesus' time? You see, a donkey was known as a humble, lowly animal of peace. (Donkeys weren't used to ride into battle the way that horses were.) And since Jesus was a gentle, humble man of peace, a donkey was a perfect choice.

E is for Easter Lilies

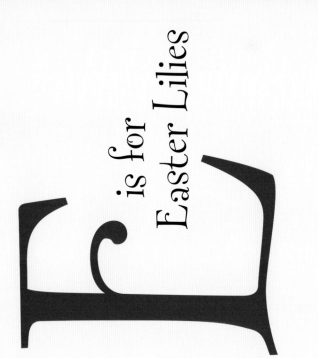

Easter lilies are, perhaps, the most famous holiday flowers of all time. Some time after Jesus' death and resurrection, some of these beautiful flowers were found growing in the Garden of Gethsemane, where Jesus went to pray the night before his crucifixion. Legend has it that these flowers sprung up where drops of Jesus' sweat fell, as He prayed and became very sad about what was happening to Him.

Here are a few hints to help you recognize which flowers are Easter lilies: These flowers have long, pointy green leaves and trumpet-shaped flowers with big, pure-white blossoms. These beautiful blossoms remind us of the pure, new life we can enjoy because of Jesus' resurrection.

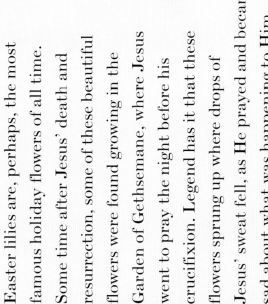

Easter is probably the world's most flexible holiday! It always happens on a Sunday, but *which* Sunday is a different story every year! Easter can pop up on the calendar on any Sunday between March 22 and April 25. For example, in 2008 Easter will be on March 23, while in 2011 it won't happen until April 24.

Have you ever wondered why Easter doesn't fall on the same date every year, like Christmas? Here's the reason: Easter Sunday is the first Sunday after the first full moon—following the first day of spring. That's a little complicated, isn't it? That's OK. That's why we have calendars.

By the way, have you ever wondered where the name of this flexible holiday came from? Some scholars and historians believe the word Easter comes from the early-German word "eostarun," which means dawn. Just as the dawn marks the beginning of a new day, Easter marks the dawn of new hope—hope of eternal life and forgiveness from sin, all because of what Jesus accomplished on the first-ever Easter long, long ago.

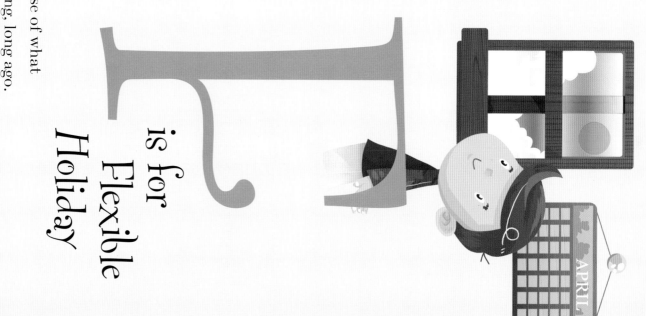

is for
Flexible
Holiday

is for Good Friday

Good Friday observes Jesus' death on the cross. Some churches hold a service from noon to 3 o'clock in the afternoon! Have you ever been to a three-hour church service? This extra-long service symbolizes the last three hours of darkness and suffering during Jesus' painful death on the cross.

Have you ever wondered why a Friday that is about Jesus' death is called "Good"? Well, some people believe that the first Christians called the day "God's Friday," and the name eventually morphed into Good Friday. Others think that "Good" refers to the blessings that we all have because Jesus loves us so much that He died for us.

H is for Hot Cross Buns

Have you ever eaten hot cross buns—during Easter, or at any time of the year? Do you remember the nursery rhyme about this sweet? A hot cross bun is a cake or biscuit with the imprint of a cross of white icing on top of it. These buns were first baked long ago in England, and they were to be eaten only on Good Friday, in honor of Jesus' death on the cross.

Today, hot cross buns are enjoyed throughout the Easter season, and, for some, all year round. After all, the spirit of the Easter season can be celebrated any time!

I is for Infant

Jesus was 33 years old when He was crucified and rose from the dead, but He first came to earth as a tiny infant. When an infant is born, he or she weighs only about 7 pounds—about as much as a house cat—and is completely helpless. An infant needs parents for protection and food.

Jesus chose to come to earth as a tiny baby so that He could grow up and experience what it's like to be human—even to the point of dying. (If He had stayed up in heaven with God, His heavenly Father, He wouldn't have ever died.) So when you pray to Jesus, you're talking to someone who knows what it's like to be you. He knows how you feel; He understands you. And, most important, He loves you.

is for Joseph of Arimathea

Because Jesus didn't worry about earning lots of money during His life, He didn't have a family burial plot in which to be laid to rest.

A wealthy man named Joseph of Arimathea (not the same Joseph who was Jesus' earthly father) was one of Jesus' followers. He respected Jesus so much that he provided a tomb for his Lord to be buried in.

But, in reality, he didn't have to give Jesus the tomb; Jesus only borrowed it. He rose from the tomb on the third day after His death, making Joseph perhaps the only person in history who found himself with a "slightly used" tomb on his hands!

K is for King Edward

Ever wonder who came up with the idea of dyeing eggs and giving them as gifts at Easter time? A painter, perhaps? A cook? A really creative kid? Actually, we might have a king to thank for this custom. Way back in the year 1290, King Edward I of England bought 450 eggs and ordered them to be decorated with bright, joyful colors. Some of the eggs were even covered with real gold. Once the eggs were properly decorated, King Edward gave them to the many members of his Royal Household.

Of course, some people believe that the Easter egg tradition was begun long before King Edward. You'll learn more about this when you get to letter "S."

is for Lent

Lent is a period of about 40 days before Easter Sunday. (Some believers celebrate Lent longer than others.) Many people who believe in God use the days of Lent to prepare for Easter—and as a time to show sorrow for the things they've done wrong and seek God's loving forgiveness. Some people even fast, limiting the kinds or amounts of food they eat during Lent. Lent is patterned after the 40 days that Jesus prayed and fasted in the wilderness as He prepared to teach and lead His people. Can you think of ways you would like to use Lent to prepare your mind and heart for Easter?

M is for Maundy Thursday

Maundy Thursday isn't the name of a singer; it's another name for Holy Thursday—which is the day before Good Friday. Maundy Thursday recalls Jesus' last meal with His disciples and His command for them to love each other. (Maundy is a Latin word that means "command.") In some churches, the priests obey this command by washing the feet of 12 church members—or poor people from their town. This ceremony helps people remember how Jesus humbly washed the feet of His 12 disciples at His final meal.

You probably don't want to go around washing people's feet, but can you think of other ways to show kindness to those around you—during Easter time and all year round?

N is for Nails

The death that Jesus died on the cross, called crucifixion, was very painful. One reason crucifixion was so excruciating is that the crucified person's hands and feet were nailed to a cross. In Old England, it became customary for blacksmiths to refuse to hammer nails into horseshoes on **Good Friday.** Household chores that used nails were also put aside until another day. This custom was adapted to show respect for Jesus and the pain **He** endured to die for our sins. Can you think of something you can do—or not do—to show your respect for Jesus on **Good Friday?**

O is for Oberammergau

Even if you know a LOT about Easter, you've probably never heard this word before. It's hard to spell—and even harder to say. *Oberammeragau* is a city in southern Germany, and it's home to the most famous Passion Play in the world. A Passion Play is a performance of the Easter story. Maybe you've seen a Passion Play in your church or at a performing arts center in your town. Passion Plays have been performed ever since the Middle Ages, and the one in Oberammeragau has been presented ever since the year 1634. This particular version of the Passion Play involves so many performers, costumes, and sets that it's presented

"Oberammeragau Passion Play... coming in 10 years!"

only once every 10 years or so. But it's worth the wait. So if you ever happen to be in Oberammeragau, Germany, during Easter, be sure to check it out!

P is for Pascha

In some European countries, Easter is called Pascha. Pascha comes from the Hebrew "pesah," which means Passover. Shortly before He was arrested and sentenced to be crucified, Jesus celebrated the Jewish festival of Passover with His closest friends. Some Christians call Easter *Pascha* because they believe that Easter—like Passover, when Jews were rescued from slavery—is a time of rescue. In this case, the rescue that is celebrated is the rescue from the power that death holds over us. Because Jesus rose from the dead and now lives forever, that means that we can too!

Q is for Quake

At the moment Jesus died on the cross, the earth quaked, shaking so hard that huge rocks were split apart! Even tombs broke open, and the bodies they contained were raised to life.

This all happened to give everyone a preview of Jesus' great resurrection, which was yet to come. When the soldiers guarding Jesus witnessed the great earthquake, even they were terrified. One of their leaders said, "Surely He [Jesus] was the Son of God!"

R is for Resurrection

Without Jesus' resurrection from the dead, there would be no Easter and no hope of eternal life. When people talk of Jesus' being resurrected, they mean that His dead body became alive again, stronger than it ever was before—a body that couldn't become sick and would never grow old. What does the resurrection mean for you? It means that if you accept Jesus into your heart, you will live forever in a marvelous body just like His!

In Eastern European countries, people get so excited about the resurrection that they greet each other by saying, "Christ is risen!" Then, the people who receive that first greeting respond with one of their own: "He is risen indeed!" Then, the people usually exchange kisses on the cheek.

You might want to avoid the kissing part, but this Easter, greet someone with "Christ is risen!" and see if he or she knows how to respond.

is for Symbol

Easter is a highly symbolic holiday. Throughout this book, you can read about many of the symbols connected to the Easter season. What is a symbol, anyway? A symbol is when one thing represents, or reminds us of, another thing. For example, the cross on the top of the hot cross buns you read about back in letter "H," symbolizes the cross that Jesus died on. And here's one more Easter symbol for you: After Jesus died and rose again, his friend Mary Magdalene had the chance to visit a powerful leader named Emperor Tiberias. Tradition has it that when Mary met Tiberias, she gave him a red-dyed egg as a symbol of Jesus' resurrection. Just as a bird can burst from an egg and later fly into the sky, Jesus rose from the dead and ascended into heaven.

Before He was arrested, Jesus got to enjoy a rare time of honor and celebration. Five days before Passover, He made a triumphant entry into the city of Jerusalem, riding on a donkey. Many of the people in Jerusalem were so thrilled to see Him that they spread palm branches and clothing in His path. (It was their version of the "Red Carpet," which you might see movie stars or political leaders walking on.) Jesus' followers also shouted things like: "Blessed is He who comes in the name of the Lord!" "Blessed is the King of Israel!" and "Hosanna! Hosanna is a Hebrew expression that means "Save!" The people shouted this because they knew Jesus could save them from their sins.

Today, we celebrate Jesus'
Triumphal Entry on Palm Sunday, which is the Sunday before Easter—and the first day of what is called Holy Week. The name "Palm Sunday" was inspired by the palm branches used to carpet Jesus' path.

T is for Triumphal Entry

U is for Unique

Easter is a unique event in human history. Jesus came to earth as God in human form. But He didn't come to earth to control the world like a political leader or perform feats of strength like a superhero so that He could impress everyone. He came to serve people, to love people, to heal people who were sick and hurt. And He came to die to pay for everyone's sins.

That's what makes Easter, and Jesus, unique.

V is for Victory

Every Easter we celebrate Jesus' victory. He earned victory over death, giving all people hope that, even if they die, they can come back to life if they have believed in Him. Jesus also scored a victory over sin when He was raised from the dead. When He was crucified, Jesus took on Himself all of the sins of the world—sins that would keep people from living in heaven and having a close relationship with God. This means that Jesus took the punishment for every wrong thing you have ever done—and ever will do. So you don't have to worry about God holding your sins against you. You are forgiven for everything. Now, that's a victory worth celebrating at Easter, and every day!

W is for Wednesday

In many churches, a special Wednesday, called Ash Wednesday, begins the Lent season. Some churches hold a service on Ash Wednesday, and one of the customs during this service is for a minister to dip one finger into a dish filled with ashes, then dab the ash on the foreheads of the people. Sometimes the minister will draw a small cross with the ashes. This ceremony is designed to help people begin Lent with a humble spirit. (In the earliest biblical times, people put ashes on their head to show they were sorry for something they did or to show they were sad about something.)

is for...Christ

No, those words up there aren't mistakes. Now, the word "Christ" doesn't start with **X**, and neither does "Jesus" or "Messiah." But early Christians used **X** as a symbol for Christ. That's why you sometimes see "**X**mas" used as a shorter way of writing "Christmas." And remember the Ash Wednesday custom you read about just a little while ago? Well, sometimes on Ash Wednesday, a minister will use ashes to draw an **X** on someone's forehead as a reminder that Christ is the reason we celebrate the Easter Season.

is for Yahweh (Yah-way)

Yahweh is the Hebrew word for God. When people like Abraham, David, and Moses prayed to God, they called Him Yahweh. All of the events of Easter were part of Yahweh's plan. Still, it had to be so painful for Him to watch His beloved son die. (Think of how you feel when you must watch a parent, friend, or sibling suffer.) God's suffering was extra difficult because He had the power to stop Jesus from being killed. But He knew that if Jesus didn't take on the punishment for all of humanity's sins, the people wouldn't be able to handle that punishment by themselves. So, painful as it was, God allowed His son to suffer so that all of us can have eternal life and be forgiven for all we have done wrong. This Easter, take time to thank Yahweh for being willing to sacrifice His son for your sake.

Zechariah was a prophet and priest who lived more than 500 years before Jesus was even born. However, through God's power, Zechariah was able to see into the future—including some things about the very first Easter. For example, Zechariah knew that Jesus would make his Triumphal Entry into Jerusalem riding on a donkey, and not just any donkey. Zechariah proclaimed that Jesus would enter the city on a colt, a young donkey. And that's exactly how it happened!

The donkey prophecy is only one of many that Zechariah made about Jesus. He also prophesied about the lowly circumstances of Jesus' birth, how He would be arrested and killed, and His eternal reign in heaven. And every one of Zechariah's prophecies came true!

Z is for Zechariah

A final note about Easter . . .

Now that you know Easter from A to **Z**, perhaps this wonderful season will be extra meaningful to you. Always remember that Easter is a time for celebrating the hope and new life that we have, thanks to Jesus' power, and Jesus' great love.

If you have enjoyed this book,
Hallmark would love
to hear from you.

Please send comments to

Book Feedback
2501 McGee, Mail Drop 215
Kansas City, MO 64141-6580

Or e-mail us at

booknotes@hallmark.com